AF574857

TALES OF AWE AND WONDER

TALES OF AWE AND WONDER

OUR MEDIEVAL HERITAGE

JOHANNA O'MAHONY WALTERS

VERITAS

First published 2000 by
Veritas Publications
7-8 Lower Abbey Street
Dublin 1

Copyright © 2000 Johanna O'Mahony Walters

All rights reserved. No part of any contribution to this volume may be reproduced, stored in a retrieval system, or transmitted, in any form or by any means, electronic, mechanical, photocopying, recording, or otherwise without the prior permission of the copyright holder.

ISBN 1 85390 469 4

British Library Cataloguing
in Publication Data.
A catalogue record for
this book is available
from the British Library.

Designed by Bill Bolger
Illustrations by Jeannette Dunne
Printed in the Republic of Ireland by Betaprint Ltd, Dublin

Norway
Sweden
Margaret of Scotland
1046–1093
United Kingdom
Denmark
Ireland
Julian of Norwich
1342–1416 AD
London
Netherlands
Mechtilde of Magdeburg
1212–1282 AD.
BERLIN
ERFURT
Germany
Meister Eckhart
1260–1327 AD
Belgium
Hildegarde of Bingen
1098–1179 AD.
PARIS
Bernard of Clairvaux
1045–1093 AD.
France
Hungary
Catherine of Siena
1347–1380 AD.
1181–1226 AD.
ST. Francis
ST. Clare
1196–1253 AD.
Italy
ASSISI
St. Dominic
1170–1221 AD.
Palencia
Madrid
Spain
Monte Cassino Abbey
Rome
ST. Benedict
480–550 AD.
Aquino
St. Thomas Aquinas
1225–1274 AD.
Portugal
N
W
E
S

Thanks to my friend Jean Francis who supported this book through to its publication. Her advice, editing skills and constant encouragement are much appreciated. Thanks also to David and Neil, to my friends Jacqui, Eleanor, Eileen and Mercy B for their love and support.

I dedicate this book to the memory of my parents,
Neil and Nora O'Mahony.

CONTENTS

Timeline

Taken from *The Universe Story* by Brian Swimme and Thomas Berry

If the whole history of the universe were to be condensed into one day, we humans would have arrived in the last half hour. Isn't that a sobering thought?

According to Thomas Berry, the universe is fifteen billion years old and the first humans appeared 2.6 million years ago. We are indeed a very young species. The following timeline begins with the discovery of fire.

32,000 years ago	Fireplace cooking. Lamps. Cave art.
20,000 years ago:	Well-crafted decorated spears. Beaded and fitted clothing.
12,000 years ago:	Beginning of Neolithic Age.
10,000 – 5,000 years ago:	Animals – dogs, goats, pigs – and plants,– wheat, barley, rice – are domesticated. Grasp of seasonal cycles. Pottery. Weaving. Mother goddess shrines.
5,000 – 2,500 years ago:	Ancient civilisations – Sumer, Babylon, Egypt. Irrigation. The wheel. Writing. Rise of male deities.
2,500 – 2,000 years ago:	Buddha. The Upanishads. The Roman Empire. Jesus.
400 AD	The Fall of Rome. Europe enters the Dark Ages.
900 – 1485 AD	Medieval Europe — The Middle Ages
480 – 550 AD	Benedict.
1046 – 1093 AD	Margaret of Scotland.
1098 – 1179 AD	Hildegarde of Bingen

1170 – 1221 AD	Dominic
1181 –1226 AD	Francis of Assisi
1196 – 1253 AD	Clare of Assisi
1212 – 1282 AD	Mechtilde of Magdeburg
1225 – 1274 AD	Thomas Aquinas
1260 – 1327 AD	Meister Eckhart
1342 – 1416 AD	Julian of Norwich
1347 – 1380 AD	Catherine of Siena
500 years ago:	Earth is a sphere. Planets revolve around the sun. Science to subdue nature.
400 – 200 years ago:	Gravity. Anatomy. Zoology. Geology. Nation States. Industrial Revolution. Pollution.
Less than 100 years ago:	New understanding of our cosmic story — an evolving interconnected universe.
Now:	You are here — a part of the story. The universe becoming aware of its own story.

INTRODUCTION

Mystics are people who have complete union with God; they don't see themselves as separate from God or from anybody or anything else, they see themselves as part of the whole. We are all born mystics and I feel sure that you are all still mystics. If we live in the now, and do not spend our time looking forward to whatever it is that will happen in the future, or looking back to whatever happened last year or last month, there is a fair chance that we might still be mystics. Creative people such as artists, poets, etc., actually work from mystical experience – a deep sense of knowing, a closeness to nature, a feeling of connectedness to the universe and to all of life.

Now these are not extraordinary beings, they are just like you and me. The medieval mystics that you will read about here were people of their time. They lived in the Middle Ages, a period that is known as medieval (except for Benedict, who lived in the Dark Ages, after the fall of Rome in 410, a time when the Celtic monks and nuns kept the spirituality of Christianity alive.) The names and ways of these mystics may seem a little strange to us, but no doubt in nine hundred years' time people will find our ways and names a little strange!

Some were fat, some were thin, some were short and some were tall. They had their stubborn ways like we often have. They were their own people and when they wanted something they just went for it regardless. They were strong characters who were not afraid to speak the truth about the times. If they thought something was corrupt they would say so, and they often got into trouble for it. Nobody could call them fainthearted. They really lived life to the full. They did not see life as trivial and neither should we. Life is for living; it is a great adventure. So turn off the television, there is no need to watch the characters in the soaps living their lives when you are such a special, unique and interesting person yourself.

People with faith play and have fun, others have to be more serious and make a chore out of everything. You will notice that the people you will read about here were joyful people who had a lot of fun, life for them was an adventure.

BENEDICT

Benedict was a young Italian boy, who liked the outdoor life. He had a twin sister called Scholastica, and they spent a lot of time together, exploring the local countryside. They loved the mountains and rivers and enjoyed the singing of the birds. They also liked the peace and quiet of the countryside and both learnt to spend long periods in silence.

Benedict, though he was a very intelligent young man, was very humble. He never boasted about his great knowledge, and even though he was good at sport, he never showed off. He was always ready to help the other boys of his age.

When Benedict was fourteen years old he went to Rome to study. It was quite common in the Middle Ages for young boys and girls to leave their homes and go off to study with renowned scholars at large centres of learning. He was not happy in Rome; he was shocked by the rather wicked way people lived there. This was in the Dark Ages when Europe was in a state of chaos after the fall of the Great Roman Empire. Rome itself was in the hands of savage hordes called Barbarians who attacked the city. Benedict left Rome to live a simple life in the mountains where a monk called Romanus, from one of the local monasteries, looked after him. He ate a plain diet of berries and fruit that grew locally. When he was twenty he became a hermit in one of the mountain caves about forty miles east of Rome.

He attracted many disciples, whom he organised into twelve small monastic communities scattered around the mountains. He wrote a simple rule of life for his monks, called *The Little Rule for Beginners.* He saw this as an example rather than a blueprint for the monastic life. He had no idea how important this rule was to become. It became the pattern for the way monks lived throughout the whole of Europe. It was made up of an equal balance of prayer, work and study. The monks were allowed to wear clothing suitable to the season and were able to have seven or eight hours of sleep every night. So as you can see it was quite a sensible rule, which is why it has survived to this day.

But like many really good people, Benedict had enemies, people who were jealous of him. One day somebody tried to kill him by offering him a drink that had poison in it. Fortunately, he had only taken one sip when he realised that something was wrong. He left his mountain hermitage and went off to Monte Cassino where he founded the famous Benedictine monastery, which is about halfway between Rome and Naples. Again his kind and gentle ways attracted many young men who came and joined him.

Benedict was a modest and compassionate man who ruled his monasteries with wisdom and loving-kindness. He insisted that the monks maintain their

regular practice of work, prayer and study, which he called their discipline. The respect he had for others made him a wonderful spiritual father to his community. To this day he is regarded as the father of monasticism.

His sister Scholastica founded the order of Benedictine nuns who lived by the rule her brother had written.

The Benedictine monasteries became great centres of learning. Benedict is considered to be the patron saint of schoolchildren because of the many distinguished schools the Benedictine monks have run for centuries. Pope Paul VI – who was the pope before our present pope – proclaimed him the patron saint of Europe.

We celebrate the feast of Benedict on 11 July. Even though he is not actually a medieval saint, he is very important to the Middle Ages because of the monastic foundations that he established, which helped the Church to grow steadily.

Let's Contemplate Darkness

We talked about the Dark Ages when there was a lack of order in Europe as a result of the fall of the Roman Empire. People were very fearful about what might happen to them, and they were distrustful of everybody and everything. When they went to bed each night they did not know what the next day would bring, or what enemies might pound on their doors in the middle of the night. They lay awake frightened of the darkness of the night and the darkness that seemed to be overwhelming Europe.

Are you afraid of the dark?

There really is no need to fear the dark. Sit quietly in a darkened room for about fifteen minutes – what do you notice?

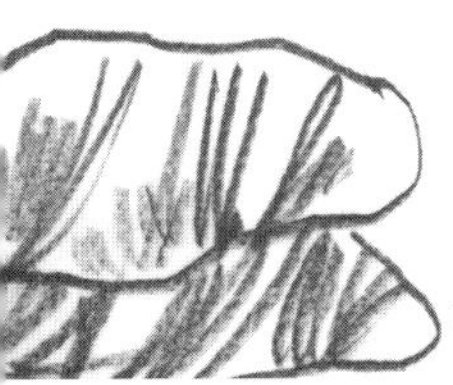

We actually grow strong in the darkness. We lived very safely and grew very strong and healthy in the safety of our mother's tummy for nine months before we made our dramatic entrance into this world of light and sound.

Observe the seeds we put into mother earth. If we left them on top of the ground, would they grow? They need the darkness deep in the soil to form strong and healthy roots to help them make their journey towards the sun. Plant a seed in the ground and observe how it grows and develops. How long does it take to grow into a strong and tall plant?

Sometimes in our lives we have what we call a dark time when we feel sad and weary and when nothing appears to be working out for us. Be patient and know that you are growing and unfolding as God intended you to. We need darkness in our lives just as we need light, but the light seems to be more popular. In the cycle of the year notice how we go from light to darkness and back again to light; in the course of a day we go from day to night and back to day – it is a constant flow from one to the other. In the darkness we can rest. If we do not get a good night's sleep we do not have the energy to do all the things we need to do in the daytime. During the winter, nature sleeps. The seeds are deep in the earth safe from the cold and the wind, and many of the animals are sleeping also.

Make a list of all the animals you know of who hibernate.

Do you play an instrument? If so, you could compose some 'Night Music' or you could write a poem 'In Praise of the Dark'.

Collect some night-time pictures and use them to make a collage.

BERNARD OF CLAIRVAUX

BERNARD was born near Dijon in Burgundy, in a very beautiful wine-producing region of France. His family was rich and powerful so he had quite a comfortable and privileged life as a young boy. He had five brothers and one sister, with whom he enjoyed playing and making up games to play outdoors. This is an interesting quotation from Bernard:

Believe me, for I know
You will find something far greater
In the woods than in books.
Stones and trees will teach you
That which you cannot learn from the Masters.

He lived in a time when the poor could not say what they felt and were often victims of the cruelty and selfishness of the rich. Bernard was a shrewd young man who observed this state of affairs. It troubled him and he often discussed it with his father who was a just and fair man. He treated his workers well. In this way Bernard developed a deep respect for mercy, justice and fair play and he had a loyal affection for others. He was the kind of boy you would like to have for a friend. He was very straightforward and honest without being a 'holy Joe'.

As he was a great scholar, who had a talent for writing, he went off to pursue his studies for the priesthood. He was extremely well educated with an interest in literature, science and the arts. Unfortunately, his mother died and he was so sad and upset by her death that he gave up his literary studies, and, although given a chance of promotion within the Church, he went off to live alone in the woods. He went to visit the Cistercian monastery at Citeaux and sought the advice and spiritual help of the abbot. He persuaded his brother and twenty-five other young men, who were very intelligent like himself, to join the monastery and help to reform it. They lived there by the Rule of St Benedict.

Bernard showed his love for God by extreme fasting and lack of sleep, which affected his health – he suffered from migraines, anaemia and tummy upsets. You can imagine how difficult it must have been to live the life of a monk, engaging in prayer, work and study when he did not feel well. He and his friends managed to turn the monastery at Citeaux into a thriving community which, through hard work, expanded and grew.

In 1115 he went off with a small group of monks to establish a new monastery at Clairvaux. Four of his brothers, an uncle and a cousin joined them, but it took well over ten years to make the monastery pay for itself. In his first years as abbot of Clairvaux he was strict in the practice of the rule, but, with time and ill health, he mellowed and slackened his strict regime. He remained abbot of Clairvaux until his death in 1153.

As Bernard's health worsened, his spirituality deepened. He retired to a hut near the monastery and there he lived for the rest of his life. It has been said that due to his tummy problems he suffered from halitosis, which means he had really bad breath, and that it was out of consideration for the other monks that he moved! He lived a truly mystical prayer life and he was an

eloquent preacher – people came from all over Europe to hear him. He was the most famous monk of his time.

He has left many writings on the spiritual and monastic life. He wrote beautiful poetry and books about Mary, the mother of God. He wrote more than three hundred letters and sermons. These show how he tried to combine a mystical life – a total absorption in God – with his love and concern for those who lived in misery, and his concern for the monks in his care and the great responsibility he had for their welfare. Towards the end of his life he spent more and more time in the woods beside his hut, enjoying the singing of the birds.

Let's Contemplate Birds

One hundred and fifty million years ago the sound of birdsong was heard on earth for the very first time. We humans only arrived on planet earth about two and a half million years ago. So you can see we are relative newcomers compared with our feathered friends.

Did you ever wonder what our planet home would be like without the song of the birds? I think it would be a very lonely place. They really do delight us with their wonderful music. The amazing thing is that they all sound so different. Are you able to recognise the different songs of the birds? Have you any idea how many different species of birds there are? Their array of colour and beauty is a joy to behold. Why do we take these fragile and beautiful creatures for granted? We may be the last generation who will hear birdsong because their habitats are being destroyed. How does that make you feel?

Remember how your mother prepared a cosy and warm room for you, a place where you could be safe and warm? Can you think of ways you can make the world a safer place for birds? How can we protect their home from destruction? Remember to feed them especially in winter.

Go for a walk today and listen to the birds sing to you, and notice how different their songs are.

When the birds fly south in the winter, how do they know the way? Could you find your way to Africa? It is miraculous how these tiny, fragile creatures can travel that huge distance and find their way back again to your garden the following spring. Close your eyes and really think about this awesome truth.

Think about how little a bird eats. On a few grains of corn they can fly high into the sky and sing their little hearts out.

Could you try to imitate the songs of the birds? Perhaps you could make a tape and call it 'A Bird Symphony'.

Many people have composed songs about birds, can you think of any? Make a list of songs and rhymes about birds. Perhaps you could ask your mother or father to help you. Perhaps you could make up a rhyme or song of your own about your favourite bird, you might also like to draw a picture of it.

MARGARET OF SCOTLAND

MARGARET was a princess, who was born and brought up at the Hungarian Court. Her father was 'Edward the Exile', who had to leave England and go into exile in Hungary during the reign of the Danish kings in England.

Margaret was a very attractive girl, she was short and dark, with a bubbly personality. She loved nice clothes and often entertained other members of the royal family with her fashion parades, when she modeled beautiful gowns for them.

She was a very intelligent girl who had her own private tutor at court. She enjoyed reading and making music. She was so devout and prayerful that many people thought she might become a nun. She had all she wanted, she only had to ask and her slightest wish was granted. What a lucky girl!

When she came on a visit to Scotland the king saw her and fell madly in love with her, and she with him. Soon they were married. It sounds like a fairy story, and perhaps it was. They made a very handsome couple who were good and kind to the people. They ruled Scotland wisely and well. She helped her husband with all his kingly duties and the people loved her. She used to go out among the poor people giving them food and gifts. Her spare time she spent in reading, praying and making beautiful vestments for the Church. She was an excellent seamstress.

During her reign as queen of Scotland, she brought about a lot of reform in the Church, and took a prominent part in the foundation of monasteries, churches and hostels for pilgrims. During the Middle Ages, going on pilgrimages was a very popular practice, it has now been replaced by package tours! She was responsible for the revival of the abbey on the island of Iona, which is still a very popular place of pilgrimage today. She had Dunfermline Abbey built as a burial place for Scotland's royal family, rather like Westminster Abbey in London, which houses the bones of the English royal family.

Margaret had a strong influence over her husband, the king, and some of his advisers did not like this, as it curbed their power somewhat. They had eight children. Two of their sons, Alexander and David, became kings of Scotland and their daughter, Matilda, married Henry I of England.

At the age of forty-seven Margaret died. Her feastday is kept on 16 November. Saint Margaret and Saint Andrew are the patron saints of Scotland.

Let's Contemplate Our Talents

What is it that you are good at? Do you sing well? Can you dance, paint, act, play a musical instrument or model with clay or wood? Be certain that you do have a talent. Some people are good cooks, some are very hospitable – they make other people feel welcome and at ease. Maybe your talent is that you are a good listener, or perhaps you are a good friend. Are you good at sport? This gift that you offer to the community is unique, it is what makes you the person that you are. Cherish and honour it. Boast about it – but not too much or people will say you are a big-head! Give thanks for this gift because it is freely given and use it to bring joy to all around you.

Close your eyes and think about your particular gift. Contemplate the joy this gift gives to others – does it make them happy, fill them with awe perhaps or inspire them to develop their own particular talent? Offer thanks to the creator for this gift and use it for your own delight and to give delight to others.

Write a letter to a friend telling them how much you appreciate their particular gift. With a group of friends perhaps you could go to a children's hospital or an old people's home and share your gift with the people there and encourage them to share their talents with you. Would this not be a wonderful exchange of gifts?

HILDEGARDE OF BINGEN

HILDEGARDE was a very important German lady. She was born in 1098. She was the youngest of ten children. Her parents were rich and important people. As a child she was afflicted with fragile health and always felt she was different from others. She had strange visions and could foresee future events, very mundane things like the arrival of visitors at her home. So as you can imagine the other children of her age thought her quite odd.

There was a Benedictine monastery near her home where her cousin, Blessed Jutta, lived as an anchoress in a hermitage attached to the monastery. When Hildegarde was only eight years old she went to live with this lady in her hermitage, which was later to become a convent.

This was not unusual for young girls at this time. Many were attracted to the religious life and went off to convents at a very early age. It was very unlike today's society, then girls had two choices, they either became nuns or they got married. They could not remain single and just do a job, as many girls choose to do nowadays.

When Hildegarde was fifteen years old she became a Benedictine nun. When Blessed Jutta, who was the mother superior (as the leader of the community was called) died, Hildegarde became mother superior.

She was a very talented lady, she wrote great poetry, composed music and had a wonderful knowledge of science and medicine. She also wrote some theological books. Have you seen any CDs of her chants in the music shops?

She dictated her revelations, called *Living Light,* to a monk called Volmer, who believed that it was God who spoke through Hildegarde. Even though she suffered from poor health and was plagued by migraines, she became very famous as a healer and visionary and many people sought her help and advice. Some of these people were very important – kings, queens, abbots, monks, nuns and many ordinary people.

When Hildegarde died in 1179 she was one of the best-known women in all of Germany. 1998 was the nine-hundredth anniversary of her birth. There were celebrations in her honour all over the world and her music was played and sung.

She was also famous for the love she had for the whole of creation. She knew of the sanctity of the earth and of our need to protect it. Here is one of her statements about the abuse of our planet home:

> *There is nothing in Creation which does not have some radiance, either greenness or seeds or flowers or beauty – otherwise it would not be part of Creation.*

LET'S CONTEMPLATE CREATION

Let us find ways of praising creation and finding our connectedness with it, how we are part of the web of life and how we engage with the natural world in an appropriate way.

I walk with Beauty before me
I walk with Beauty behind me
I walk with Beauty above me
I walk with Beauty below me
I walk with Beauty all around me
As I walk my life the beauty way.

A Navajo Indian composed this chant.

Observe a spider's web. Could you make one? Could you draw one?

Observe the dew on the early morning grass. See how it glistens. Write a poem about it.

Observe a ladybird on a leaf.

Listen to the birds sing. Can you hear a bee buzzing?

Smell the grass, the roses, the honeysuckle and the gorse. Describe these smells. Have you got herbs in your garden such as rosemary, lavender or thyme? Try them in your cooking.

Taste the rain, fruit or vegetables growing in your garden (wash them first, they may have been sprayed).

Walk barefoot in your garden and feel the grass under your feet. You can also dance out of doors in your bare feet. How does it feel?

DOMINIC

DOMINIC was born in a small town in northern Spain. His parents, Felix and Jane de Guzman, were a handsome and very rich young couple. Dominic was a beautiful baby with the most amazing brown eyes. The summers were very warm and the winters very cold in this mountainous region of Spain.

Dominic was good at sport, he could outrun any of his brothers but he preferred to read and spent much of his time reading with his mother. She had taught him to read when he was quite young. He also learned his love of the poor and underprivileged from his mother, who was well respected in the area for her kindness and gentleness.

When he was only seven years old, Dominic's parents decided that he was to become a priest so they sent him off to another town, where he attended a school that was run by his uncle. He was really sad to be leaving home, especially being parted from his mother whom he loved so much. Being a good student and having a lively personality, he got on well at the school, the other boys liked him and when they were not studying they had a lot of fun together.

At the age of fifteen he went off to college at a place called Palencia. Here he excelled at his studies and won a reputation as a great scholar. Many people thought that he would one day be a bishop. Here too, people noticed his great love and concern for the poor and his love of prayer; he would often spend whole nights in prayer.

Next Dominic went off to a city called Osma, to a college beside the cathedral, which had a small school attached to it. A man called Diego was the Bishop of Osma at that time and he and Dominic became very close friends. When the bishop was sent on a royal mission abroad, he took Dominic with him. While on the journey, they became aware of a threat to the Church by a group of heretics in the South of France. They were teaching a strange doctrine that whatever concerned the body – eating, drinking, etc., was bad and had to be renounced in favour of a very strict regime in which the body was to be punished. The pope was very worried about this teaching, so he asked Dominic and the bishop to help him curb the heretics. They felt that the only way of winning the heretics back was by the example of preachers who lived very simple lives themselves, men who would tramp the roads barefoot and in poverty, so that is how Dominic started off the Dominican Order of Preachers. To this day they are called OPs, which is short for Order of Preachers.

Dominic then established a convent, formed from a group of women converted from the heresy.

Eventually a war broke out between the pope and the followers of the heresy. The pope won and Dominic and his friends were firmly established as preachers. From then on, his idea of an order devoted to preaching developed quickly. He told the pope of his plan and the pope advised him to adopt the rule of an existing order.

Around this time Dominic met Francis of Assisi and the two of them became great friends. They were similar in many ways – they were both idealistic, intelligent young men with a great love for the less fortunate. Francis was concerned with feeding and caring for the poor, with whom he identified. Dominic concerned himself with preaching and teaching people who otherwise would not have had an opportunity to get an education. They were the first of what came to be known as the mendicant orders - monks who went out and about among the people, like their predecessors the Celtic monks. Before this, since the time of Benedict, monks had lived in monasteries and people had come to them.

Eventually Dominic adopted the Rule of St Augustine. The houses he established became schools of theology, which later became the first universities.

Dominic had a clear vision of what he wanted his communities to be. His followers respected him for his gentle way of dealing with people.

In about 1218 he went on a long journey, travelling about 3,380 miles entirely on foot. He went from Rome to Toulouse in France, then to Spain and all the way back again to Rome via Paris and Milan. I wonder how long it took him! His health began to fail but he continued his work joyfully until the

end. On 6 August 1221 he died very quietly, surrounded by his monks at their house in Bologna. The Dominican Order went from strength to strength. Do you know any Dominican priests, nuns or brothers? Perhaps you could find out if there is a priory near your home. You will recognise the monks by their white clothes, which are called habits.

Let's Contemplate Change

Without change we do not grow or develop. Can you imagine, if you did not change you would still be a baby! Wouldn't that be awful? So you can see the need for change. When we are young we grow and change very rapidly, but as we get older it gets a bit more difficult. We tend to fear change. We like the familiarity of what we know. But it is really exciting to take a great leap into the unknown – often it is by doing this that we learn to fly! We become the people we were created to be. Life suddenly becomes a great and exciting adventure.

As you have just read, Dominic was prepared to leave the security of what he knew to walk the roads and go to the people rather than the other way round. This had a profound effect on the way priests and monks were perceived at that time and has left a very rich legacy for us today. The education of the ordinary people began with these adventurous monks, who became known as friars.

What would you consider a great adventure? Think about it; discuss it with your friend. What is it that is holding you back from realizing your dreams? Is it fear of the unknown? It is also important to be able to change your point of view as new ideas come to you. We cannot go through life thinking and believing the same things that we thought and believed when we were really young. It is important to have an opinion and, even if other people think it is silly or inappropriate, you stick to it if it is what you sincerely believe. You are entitled to this and people have no business to tell you otherwise.

Think about the things you have changed your mind about, things you might have thought were absolutely important, and now you hold a different opinion. What caused you to change your mind?

Now look at the changes in nature. If the seed was never put in the ground it could never change into a beautiful flower. Likewise if the leaves did not fall off the trees and go into the ground and die, the tree would not be nourished for next year's growth. Think about the importance of the seasons and why they need to change. How would we survive if they never changed?

Listen to the music 'The Four Seasons' by a composer called Vivaldi. Imagine the beauty and elegance of each season. Perhaps you could compose a dance to this music or you could get together with a group of friends and make a group dance, with a few of you representing each season and the others being perfectly still while each season does their part. Think about the value of stillness and recognize that movement comes out of the stillness, just as speech comes from silence. You could extend this dance further by incorporating poetry. Write a poem in praise of each season, and then maybe add some music to the poems. Also you could paint a picture of the four seasons showing the changes. The possibilities are endless.

FRANCIS OF ASSISI

All praise be yours my Lord, through Sister Moon and Stars;
All praise be yours my Lord, through Brothers Wind and Air;
All praise be yours my Lord, through Sister Water.

Francis was the son of a very rich merchant who lived in the town of Assisi, in Italy. He was a fun-loving boy who enjoyed all sorts of sport and often got up to mischief. He lived a very extravagant and carefree life until it was time for him to join the army and go to war.

He went off to battle with many other young men from Assisi. There was a big celebration in their honour and all the townspeople came to wish them well, thinking them very brave to be going off to defend their country.

But war changed them, especially Francis. He saw that war was not a glorious thing. It made some people very rich and others very poor and homeless. He saw how it brought out the cruel and baser side of men's natures. Neither could he bear to see so many people, who were just like himself, being killed. So he left the army and came home. He was very ill for a long time and his mother nursed him. His father was ashamed of him and called him a deserter and a coward.

Francis now saw life in a different way. He gave away all his possessions and went off to live among the poor and the sick. His father was furious because he gave away so much of his beautiful fabrics and possessions to the poor. Francis said, 'Possessions do not bring us happiness, look at my father, he has got so much and he is so miserable. Behold the lilies of the field, they neither sow nor reap and not even Solomon in all his glory was arrayed like one of these.' His father disowned him, threw him out of his house and told him he never wanted to see him again. This made his mother very sad because she loved Francis very much.

He became a travelling preacher, living like the poor, having to beg for his

food and wearing very simple and rough clothing. Strangely, after some time, many of his friends joined him – young men who had grown up with him and been in the army with him, men like himself who had once been very rich.

Nature became very important to Francis. He loved being out in the open, communing with the plants and animals with whom he knew he was connected. He referred to them as his sisters and brothers. He also referred to the sun as his brother and to the moon as his sister. Have you seen the movie 'Brother Sun, Sister Moon'? It is a very beautiful film about the life of Francis, with lovely music and magnificent scenery. The birds and animals had no fear of him, they loved him and came very close to him. The birds would sit on his hands and sing to him.

He wrote a very simple rule for himself and his brothers, who came to be known as friars. They lived a regimen of extreme poverty. But they were a very happy and joyful group of people, who expressed gratitude for all the wonderful gifts we receive daily without asking. There are thousands of Franciscan friars and nuns in the world today who follow the rule of Francis. Do you know any?

He died on 4 October 1226 and he is still remembered with love throughout the world to this day. Many people claim him as the first hippy! Do you know what a hippy is? Ask your parents! He is also considered to be the first 'green' saint. Do you think he ought to be the patron saint of the environment?

Do you know the song 'Make Me a Channel of Your Peace'? It was written in honour of Saint Francis.

Let's Contemplate the Sun

Believe it or not the sun is a star. Do you know what it is made of? Do you know the story of Icarus and Daedalus? Read the story of Icarus and Daedalus and draw a picture of it. Find out what happened to Icarus when he flew too close to the sun. Where does the sun rise and set? When does it cast its longest shadow? You can have a lot of fun with your shadow; you can chase it, measure it, try and jump on it, jump on your friend's shadow. On a nice day place a stick in an upright position in your garden, and go out every hour and put a pebble where the shadow falls. How many pebbles have you got by the end of the day? Does the sun move? It looks as if it does, but actually it is the earth that moves. Could we manage without the sun? If not, why not? Do you know what happens in countries where the sun shines all the time and where rain seldom falls? There are other parts of the world where the sun never shines for several months of the year. We are very lucky to have the climate we have, we need to be grateful to the sun for many things. Write a 'Thank You' poem to the sun. Begin each line with 'Thank you for…'

How long is your poem? Decorate it and give it as a gift to your best friend.

Our ancestors had a very special relationship with the sun. They honoured the gifts it gave them and expressed their gratitude in dance and song, creating wonderful ritual celebrations.

Do you think we take this great gift for granted?

Write a story about a girl/boy who lives in a country where the sun never shines. Try to feel what life might be like there, how everything might look, what sounds you might hear. Do you think the girl/boy would grow strong and healthy? Would they have sufficient food?

CLARE OF ASSISI

FRANCIS of Assisi had known Clare growing up, but she had always avoided him and his friends; she considered them too boisterous and selfish. She, being a conscientious and serious girl, loved the poor and the sick and every day she secretly took food to the lepers who lived on the outskirts of the town. Lepers were not allowed to go into towns or mix with other people because their illness was highly contagious and maimed them badly. Often they lost limbs as a result of it.

Clare was very beautiful and by the time she was fifteen her parents had selected a suitable husband for her from a noble family.

She had become very friendly with Francis while he was recovering from his illness and she had been captivated by his ideas. Later, she heard Francis preach and arranged a secret meeting with him. She knew for certain what she wanted to do with her life so she ran away from home. Francis met her and took her to the local Benedictine convent, where she had her beautiful long hair cut off.

As you can imagine, her family were really upset and they tried very hard to get her to come home, but she refused to return to them. She went off to live at San Damiano, which was the first church Francis had restored after his

conversion. There she stayed as an enclosed nun until the end of her life. Other young women joined her, including her sister, Agnes, and they became known as the poor ladies of Assisi. We now know them as the Poor Clares.

Francis's plan for these ladies was that they would live a public and partly travelling life, rather like the friars. People were outraged at the idea of women wandering about healing and preaching, so they wrote to the pope, who sent them a rule from Rome insisting that they become an enclosed order.

Even though Clare had a strong and close relationship with Francis, she had her own ideas on how women who became nuns ought to live. She was a great leader of people. She was otherworldly – she said 'If we have no possessions we cannot be manipulated'. Her personal life was not easy; she lived in extreme poverty, with no worldly comforts, she had a constant struggle with the pope about the rule, and she suffered from an illness that lasted for twenty-eight years. She renounced all the things that make the rest of us happy. Clare believed it was a privilege to have refused a royal marriage in order to live in poverty and discomfort for the sake of Christ.

She died in 1253. She is still remembered with great affection and many girls are called Clare in her honour.

Let's Contemplate the Moon

Slowly, silently now the Moon
Walks the night in her silver shoon
This way and that she stares and sees
Silver fruit upon silver trees.
(Walter De La Mare)

Go out on a moonlit night, how does it feel? Is the moon high in the sky? What shape is it? Is the moon always the same shape? Of what use is it? Could we manage without it? Why do you think it looks different at certain times? When do we have a full moon? The moon is said to affect our moods – do you think that is true? The moon also affects the tides, do you know how?

Do you know any poems or songs about the moon? How are we connected to it? Does it cast shadows? When you are lying in bed at night and the moonlight is streaming into your bedroom, how does that feel? Do you think it has a magical quality?

Think of some reasons why we need to be grateful to the moon. Why do you think so many poets and artists have written poetry and painted pictures of the moon? Why do we talk about the 'Man in the Moon'? People have been on the moon. Do you know the name of the first man who walked on the moon? How long ago was that? What did he say when he stepped onto the surface of the moon? How do you think he and the other two astronauts felt on that occasion?

Close your eyes and pretend you are in a spaceship, which is just about to land on the moon – countdown 10 9 8 7 6 5 4 3 2 1 – now you are there, how does it feel? What can you see? Does the landscape of the moon differ from our landscape?

Write down what you see, hear and feel. Can you taste anything? Are there any smells? Touch the ground – what does that feel like? Are you able to stand still? Why not? Can you have a drink of water?

Do you think we would be able to live on the moon? If not, why not? Why do we say the moon is made of green cheese?

Have you ever heard a piece of music called 'The Moonlight Sonata'? If you can get the record from the library, listen to it. Do you like it? Who composed it? See if you can compose a simple dance to it in praise of the moon, with a group of friends.

MECHTILDE OF MAGDEBURG

How should one live? Live welcoming to all.

WE KNOW very little of the youth and childhood of this amazing woman except that she was of noble birth and that she was born around 1210.

She was a Beguine for about forty years of her life. Beguines were women who lived lives of poverty, chastity and prayer, either in their own homes or in communities called Beguinages. Some were married, some were single and some were widowed. They either joined for a few years or, as in Mechtilde's case, for a long time. They were free to leave whenever they wished.

The Beguines were active in most European countries. In some parts of Europe there was a settlement in every town.

In those days women were either married or became nuns, so this provided a third option for women. These women enjoyed each other's company in a stimulating and intellectual environment. They engaged in spinning, brewing and handicrafts, which they could do at home. Many worked with the sick and poor in their own homes or in hospitals. Some Beguinages became schools where the local children were taught.

Mechtilde spoke out bravely about the corruption she saw in the Church at the time, and because of this she was driven from town to town.

She kept a journal throughout her life, which was later published as *The Flowing Light of the Godhead*, and in it she tells of her direct experience of God. Her imagery in this book is amazing, it is a truly mystical piece of work, which greatly influenced Meister Eckhart, about whom you will read later.

The Church felt threatened by the Beguines because of their

freedom and the fact that they made their own rules. They were condemned and some of them were burned as witches.

After the condemnation of the Beguines, Mechtilde joined the Dominican nuns at their convent in Helfta in Germany and there she stayed until her death in 1280. She has become very popular these days because of her deep spirituality, which is portrayed in her writings. Some people say that her writings were a strong influence on the poet Dante.

Let's Contemplate Unconditional Love

Love makes us brave and certainly the Beguines were very brave women. Some people say that the women's liberation movement began with them. I believe this to be so. They did not live life by anybody's script but their own, and they were totally motivated by a great love of the Divine. Mechtilde was particularly exceptional because of her wonderful writings.

Love is a word that is used very glibly these days, but what does it mean? Is it a nice feeling we have when we see somebody who is attractive to us? Is it what motivates people to do heroic deeds, or write great poetry or songs? Think about the people you love and why. Is it because they are kind to you, or because they are attractive people?

Many people go to faraway places to help people they don't know – is that love? Some people live very simple and frugal lives because they do not wish to waste the earth's resources, or they go to areas of great natural beauty to prevent trees being felled or animals being slaughtered. They do this at their own expense, often incurring great personal hardship. Is that love? Do you know the story of Diane Fossey, who went to Rwanda to take care of our ancestors, the mountain gorillas? Look in the library for her book, *Gorillas in the Mist*, or you might be able to see the video.

Love has to do with being prepared to make personal sacrifices for something that matters to us. Right now I feel we are called on to be passionate about our planet home and the beings with whom we share this home. How can we make it more comfortable for them, particularly our less fortunate fellow humans?

Love is not dependent on the return we are going to get, or on people behaving as we want them to behave. It is about being unconditional, loving without expecting any return. This isn't easy, that's why it takes courage.

'Love', according to Saint Paul, 'is patient and kind; it is never jealous; love is never boastful or conceited; it is never rude or selfish; it does not take offence, and it is not resentful.' Do you know of anybody who loves in this way? Write a letter to a friend describing this person. You could collect some natural objects, stones, pinecones, etc., and make a special gift for this person. Perhaps you could practise patience for a week, or if that is too difficult, try a day or even an hour! You could make a decision to wish everybody well and in that way build up your own ability to love unconditionally.

THOMAS AQUINAS

Sheer Joy is God's and from this Creation happens.

YOU ARE bound to have heard of Thomas Aquinas – he was one of the greatest scholars and thinkers that ever lived. He was born in 1225 in Aquino – hence his name – near Naples in Italy. He was the youngest son of Londulf, Count of Aquino. He was a most promising boy, destined for high places. He didn't engage much in sport or other boyish activities because he was so fat! The other children were inclined to make fun of him. He preferred to spend his time reading and studying – these were his favourite pastimes. He was what we might call a swot, but he was nice with it. He treated people well and had a great respect for life in all its forms. He loved the countryside and spent a lot of time alone, enjoying its beauty and wonder.

When he was only five years old he went off to the Benedictine monastery at Monte Cassino, the monastery that Benedict founded. Here of course he excelled at his studies and was destined to become a monk. His parents had high ambitions for him; they wanted him to become abbot of Benedict's famous monastery. In this way his family could improve their fortune, by having a son in such an important position. He caused quite a stir when, at the age of nineteen, he left Monte Cassino and joined the newly formed Dominican Order of Preachers which had been founded by Dominic. They were dependent on alms in order to live. After having been part of a community with the Benedictines, where he was sure of being fed and having a bed, this was a very insecure way of life. It would be like a young rich boy today running off with New Age travellers. His aristocratic family were furious with him, they had him kidnapped and imprisoned for over a year. They tried very hard to make him renounce the religious vows of celibacy, poverty and obedience that he had made as a Dominican. They even went so far as to bring a very attractive lady to his room to tempt him. Thomas used a flaming torch to get her out of his room. His sister helped him to escape, and he went off to Paris and Cologne to study under the great scholar Albert the Great. His family, especially his mother, were truly disappointed by his decision to become a Dominican.

Thomas was a huge, slow-moving man whom his fellow students nicknamed 'the dumb ox', an unkind and untrue title since he was one of the greatest scholars of his time.

He went off to teach theology at the University of Paris, which at that time was the greatest intellectual centre in Europe. He received his masters in theology from this university, before returning home to Italy where he spent the next ten years.

Thomas was much admired for his wonderful writings. He wrote about knowledge, truth, beauty, joy and justice. He started his greatest work, the *Summa Theologica* (meaning the sum total of theology) in about 1266 but he never finished it. Even in its incomplete form, the *Summa Theologica* runs to over two million words. He also wrote about forty or fifty other famous works. He had to have four secretaries to cope with all his writings and, of course, there were no typewriters or computers then so all his work had to be handwritten! While saying Mass one day he had a mysterious vision, which profoundly affected the remainder of his life. He was struck dumb and he refused to write another word except to say that all he had written seemed like straw compared to what he had seen. Many people thought he had gone mad!

He considered reason to be 'the power to grasp reality'. He felt that loving draws us more to things than knowledge does. He believed that all of life is sacred and all beings are holy, he taught us respect for the souls in animals and plants. He believed, just as the Celtic people did, in the interdependence of all things – that everything in the Universe is connected to everything else. Modern science is now recognizing this truth. He also believed that goodness is at the heart of all things. He said, 'Every truth without exception and whoever may utter it is from the Holy Spirit.' He was a brave man who was not afraid to speak his truth, even though it got him into a lot of trouble. He endured the solitude, isolation and condemnation that is the lot of all prophets, since prophets are people who meddle in order to make things right. His lifelong commitment to justice made him very much a prophet of his time. Do you know of any prophets in our time? Very

often they are people who are against the 'powers that be' because of the way they misuse power.

He was not in favour of the very harsh regimens that many of the monks of his day imposed upon themselves. They fasted to such an extent that they made themselves ill.

He died at the age of forty-nine, a short time after he had his vision. His work is still studied to this day in universities. He served God through his scholarship and through his mysticism. He is, I think, an appropriate patron for students and academics. I feel he is the patron of all who seek truth, and is that not why we are here?

Let's Contemplate Nature

One of the most important things about Thomas Aquinas was that he believed that artists explored nature to find Truth.

I wandered lonely as a cloud
That floats on high o'er vales and hills,
When all at once I saw a crowd,
A host of golden daffodils

This poem is called 'Daffodils' and it was written by a poet who lived in the Lake District in England – a place of spectacular beauty - in the early nineteenth century. His name was William Wordsworth.

Can you find this poem, or any of Wordsworth's other poems? Look in the library. Find out about his life. Perhaps you could choose some aspect of nature that is special to you – it might be a tree, or a particular flower, a stone, a whale, or some animal or even the sea. Think about it for a while. What does it mean to you? Why? Can you describe the feeling you get when you are close to this special part of nature? Now write your own poem about it.

William Blake was another famous poet and painter. What do you know of him? Look in the library or on the internet for some information about him. One of his most famous poems is called Tyger:

Tyger! Tyger! Burning bright
In the forests of the night;
What immortal hand or eye
Could frame thy fearful symmetry?

Find this poem and read it slowly and carefully and then close your eyes and 'see' the scene conjured up in this poem, then paint your impression of this poem.

William Butler Yeats is another mystical poet. Find out what you can about him and read some of his poems.

Ludwig van Beethoven was a wonderful German composer who became a professional musician at the age of eleven. His musical ability was not hampered by the deafness that he suffered from later in life. Find some of his music, particularly his symphonies, and listen to it. If you can play an instrument, perhaps you could learn to play some pieces by Beethoven. Walk along by the sea when there are not too many people on the beach and listen to the sounds. Keep these sounds in your head and when you get home perhaps you could compose your own piece of music based on what you have heard.

William Turner is perhaps the greatest eighteenth/nineteenth century landscape painter. His work, which is largely impressionist, studies light, colour and atmosphere. His work is very popular so it should be easy to find some of his paintings; the library is a good place to look if you do not live close to an art gallery.

Monet, the French impressionist painter, is also very popular; you may have seen some of his work.

Study one of his paintings and notice his use of colour.

Are there any modern painters whose work you like? Does it resemble the work of Turner or Monet in any way? Have a look at the way David Hockney paints water. Do you think he succeeds?

MEISTER ECKHART

Every single creature is full of God and is a book about God.

MEISTER Eckhart is one of my favourite people. His real name was Johannes, but he has always been called Meister, which I expect means master; this is probably because he was a teacher, and you know how respectful we have to be to teachers! He was born in Germany in 1260. As a young boy he was full of energy and he bounded around the highways and byways near his home. He loved the great rivers, especially the Rhine, where he often sailed and fished. He had a wonderful sense of humour and the other boys enjoyed his company. They often played practical jokes on each other. One day when he was out in the mountains with a group of friends, playing a form of hide and seek, he was 'on it' and all the other boys ran into hiding. As he was trying to find them, he called out and was amazed to hear his voice coming back to him. He spent the entire afternoon calling out and singing and making up poems to himself, lost in wonder at the way his voice was returning to him. The other boys grew tired waiting for him and they stole away very quietly unknown to him. So he was left out on the mountain all alone. He did not notice that it was getting dark and he had great difficulty finding his way home. His parents were very worried about him but they were also angry with him for staying out so late. I imagine he got sent to bed without any supper!

Eckhart received a very good education and was an excellent student. He admired the Dominican way of life and when he was fifteen, he joined them. He studied in Paris, the principal centre of medieval academic excellence. He got teaching posts all over Europe and was loved by his students because of his lively mind and his encouragement of them to ask questions in their quest for truth. He spoke poetically to them about the wonder and beauty of creation. He said, 'Our first experience of God is in the beauty and glory of creation itself.' He also taught his students that 'the noblest kind of knowledge is learned by living'.

He was made prior of his community at Erfurt. He was a very popular prior because of his great love and compassion, and he was also a very good manager. He had only been prior for a short time when he had to return to Paris to take up the Dominican Chair of Theology, a great honour, which Eckhart was to hold twice (Thomas Aquinas was the only other Dominican to have been afforded the same honour). Later on he was promoted by his order and given the job of overseeing women's convents in Germany. He had to look into the position of the Beguines and he found no fault with them; instead he was very impressed by their way of life and he learned much from them.

Because of his achievements, people were jealous of him, especially the Archbishop of Cologne, who was a powerful enemy indeed. He declared Eckhart a heretic. This caused amazement among the Dominicans and among his many students. He was the first major theologian to be charged with heresy under the Inquisition. Have you heard of the Inquisition? It was a dreadful investigation into heresy by which many people were tortured for their beliefs; many wise women who were knowledgeable about herbs and healing were burned as witches. The pope intervened on Eckhart's behalf and he was saved.

Eckhart pointed out that he was not introducing new ideas that were different or superior to the Catholic Church; he was within the tradition of the Church and was being misunderstood. Which is, of course, what was happening. If his accusers charged him with heresy, he charged them with stupidity!

He had a wonderful sense of the presence of God. He believed creation to be eternal because beings live in the mind of God. He said, 'The eye with which I see God is the same eye with which God sees me.' He considered God to be a great underground river that no one can dam up and that no one can stop. Like all mystics he placed great importance on creation. He felt that by being creative ourselves we change and grow and become better people. We develop what is best in other people as well as in ourselves. As it says in the Scriptures, 'By their fruits you shall know them.'

Let's contemplate our own Creativity

Our creativity is that part of all of us which is divine, or most like our Creator. We were born to create, so it is really important that we develop this part of ourselves. Young people are especially creative; as we grow older we tend to accept more easily what other people tell us. A study carried out in America some years ago showed that 80 per cent of six-year-olds were creative while only 10 per cent of forty-year-olds were. Isn't that sad? What happens to us, as we grow older? Do not let it happen to you!

What is it that you really like to do? Something that really satisfies you and you enjoy doing? My neighbour collects pebbles from the beach and makes the most wonderful pictures; he enjoys making them much more than he enjoys looking at the finished picture.

Sit very quietly and let an idea come to you. From this idea go ahead and create. Just start with the blank page and see what happens, you will be surprised by what you can do.

Perhaps you can create a beautiful picture using paint, needlecraft or some other medium. Perhaps you can compose a beautiful dance or piece of music, or write a poem or story.

You just go right ahead and do it, follow your dream and do not let anybody tell you that you cannot reach your goals, because you can. You can do or be anything you want. If you feel that one day you might be famous because of something you can create, go for it and develop that gift which you have been blest with. Our creativity is a gift and it is important that we use our gifts.

JULIAN OF NORWICH

Just as God is truly our Father
So also is God truly our Mother.

LITTLE is known of this remarkable woman, not even her name. She was born in the year 1342 somewhere in England. She was greatly influenced by the teachings of Meister Eckhart. This was a really gloomy time in which to live. England and France were engaged in a dreadful war, which lasted off and on for a hundred years. Can you imagine a quarrel lasting that long? I wonder if the people really knew what they were fighting about! Food was scarce and people did not have any work. The country had lost much of its population due to the bubonic plague, known as the Black Death. Julian lived through the Peasant's Revolt in 1369 – an uprising of the ordinary people who were dissatisfied with their conditions. Yet Julian looked at the world and said, as did the Creator, 'It is good.' She was a compassionate woman, compassionate to all beings, not only humans. She was able to live her life without the competitiveness that seems to envelop so many people. She understood that the Creator lives in all things that have been created.

She wrote cheerfully and encouraged people to look forward to better times, not only in heaven, but also here on earth. She advised people that a good way of coping with their own misfortunes was to look at their neighbours with compassion and to help those in need. In this way she managed to help people cope with the uncertainty and poverty of the time. She advised people that it is important for those of us who are prone to discouragement to recognize God in all things and know that we are loved. That is a very important message for us today – to know, as Julian believed, that God has always loved us.

She was an anchorite. Anchorites were quite common at that time, they were mostly women who took up residence in a church and took on the name of that church. They simply 'anchored' themselves there and took a vow to remain there for the rest of their lives, spending long hours in prayer. So she is called Julian of Norwich because the Church where she lived was called Saint Julian's and it was in Norwich in East Anglia. The modern equivalent of an anchorite would be a counsellor, somebody people could go to for help and advice when they have difficulties.

Many people visited Julian, the most famous being Margery Kemp, from Kings Lynn, mother of fourteen children and listed as a mystic herself.

When Julian was thirty she had a serious illness, during which she reported seeing sixteen mystical visions. She thought she was dying at this time. She wrote about these visions in a book that she called *The Book of Showings.* These visions were sixteen revelations of ways in which God loves us.

She believed that we need knowledge and information to make us wise. She said 'Between God and the Soul, there is no between.' If this is so, then we should have no difficulty trusting our own Truth.

Let's Meditate

Mystics see the world as a place in which everything is connected to everything else in one unity. Meditation is also a source of unity, because people of different faiths can all sit in silence together and be united in their meditation.

A friend of mine who is a pilot shared his experience of flying with me. He said it is an indescribable experience – 'I am up there among the clouds and a bird flies by and there is this sudden sense of 'Yes, just this bird and myself – part of the whole.' My brother, who is a sailor, tells of similar experiences when he is sailing alone at night, just himself and the stars. These are indescribable but without doubt mystical experiences. When I visited the Skellig rock off the coast of Kerry in the southwest of Ireland I was absolutely awe-struck by this wonderful rock structure which looked like a cathedral rising up out of the sea, home to 33,000 gannets who migrate every autumn and return to the same rock every spring. I had always known about bird migration, but on this particular occasion it was something very different from knowing with my head. No doubt you have had many such experiences, when you have had this deep sense of knowing that something was so, without ever having been told, knowing that you are part of something that is much greater, something that is truly magnificent and we have no words to describe such experiences.

Be Still and Know that I am God (Psalm 46)

Many people now meditate. Benedict learned meditation from the writings of John Cassian, one of the Desert Fathers and he also encouraged his monks to read his writings and practise meditation. The Desert Fathers and mothers were men and women who lived a contemplative life in the desert in the fourth and fifth centuries. They are our spiritual ancestors and they often got into trouble with the established Church! They were rather like the Celtic monks, living simple lives of prayer and work.

Meditation, which has its roots in the bible, is a wonderful way of being in touch with the divine within you. Saint Matthew in his gospel says, 'When you pray go into a room alone, shut the door and pray to your father.' Somehow, as time went by, the art of meditating in this way disappeared, but now meditation groups are starting up all over the place.

It is important to set aside a time every day to do this. I have created a sacred space in my house (all space is sacred but this is set aside especially for meditation), it is a very small space, where I know I will not be disturbed. I've got a little altar there and I light a candle and use some incense while I meditate. You can choose your own special place, perhaps your bedroom or a room that is not often used.

Sit comfortably, with your feet firmly on the floor and your back straight. You can sit cross-legged on the floor if you find that position comfortable. You need to relax completely, so make sure there is no tension anywhere in your body before you begin to meditate. Then just concentrate on your breathing for a few minutes, breathe in and out and you will notice your breathing slowing down. Then choose a mantra – a sentence that you can keep repeating, 'Be still and know that I am God' is a good one, or the one used by the World Community of Christian Meditators, 'Maranatha', which means 'Come Lord Jesus Come' or you can choose your own, some word or sentence that you feel comfortable with. You could start by just meditating for ten minutes every day and build up to twenty or thirty minutes. Also you could use some quiet music or favourite chants, for example, Taizé chants.

CATHERINE OF SIENA

CATHERINE was the twenty-fourth child of a family of twenty-five children. Can you imagine! Two football teams. Her family were very ordinary, her father was a wooldyer so although they were not very rich, they were not destitute either. She was born in Siena, in Tuscany, which is in Italy, in the year 1347, while the Black Death was raging through Europe. So as you can imagine her life cannot have been easy. She learned at an early age to fight her corner, and she was well able to hold her own in family arguments, of which I am sure there were many among such a large family. They also had a lot of fun and on the whole were a very happy family. Catherine was an extraordinary child, quite a loner in many ways, which cannot have been too easy among so many brothers and sisters. She had her favourite place where she used to go in order to be alone, it was a little bluebell wood where she sat under her own special tree and became familiar with the many beings who made their home in the wood.

She is said to have had her first mystical experience at the age of six and these continued throughout her whole life. As was the custom of the time her parents chose a husband for her, but she refused to marry him. She even cut off her beautiful long golden hair in order to make herself less attractive. Her parents were absolutely furious with her and as a punishment they made her become a servant in her own home. This meant that she had to do all the cleaning and cooking and wait hand and foot on her brothers and sisters – rather like Cinderella. She developed an inner solitude through prayer and meditation and she practised love towards her angry family by treating them as if they were the apostles!

When Catherine was in her twenties she developed smallpox, which left her very badly scarred and, of course, ruined all her chances of marriage. Ironic, really, since she had no intention of marrying anybody. It was a strange time in which to live, especially for girls and women who had to rely on their physical beauty to be married to perhaps a very ugly man! However, now that she was no longer pretty her parents allowed Catherine to join the Third Order of Dominican nuns. This meant that she did not have to live in the convent but was committed to it in some way.

She worked tirelessly with the sick and the poor and became very well respected in her home town because of her kindness to all with whom she came in contact. She had received no formal education, but had taught herself to read, so it is really surprising that she gained a reputation as a teacher. When there was a second outbreak of the Black Death in Siena she persuaded some other brave people to join her in tending to the sick and dying.

At that time the Church was becoming very powerful and unfortunately very corrupt. Catherine formed part of a powerful group of thinkers within the Church who wished to see it reformed. She got involved in clergy reform, a crusade to the Holy Land and a campaign for the return of the Pope to Rome (he was then living in Avignon in France).

She must have been an extraordinary woman because people listened to her and did what she suggested. She founded a convent and gained a reputation as a preacher. She learned to write when she was thirty years old and between then and the time that she died at the age of thirty-three she wrote nearly 400 letters, most of which were about the state of the Church. She also wrote *The Dialogue*, a debate between herself and God. Even though she had been summoned to Rome and became the confidante of those who ruled the Church, she was very troubled by the corruption she witnessed within the institution.

It seems strange to us that somebody so young, especially a woman, should gain such prominence. In 1970 she received the great honour of being proclaimed a Doctor of the Church by the then Pope – Paul VI.

Let's Contemplate Justice

In spite of her youth, Catherine achieved a great deal in her life by bringing about justice and reform within the society in which she lived. How can we relate this to our time and the place where we live?

Is it fair that almost two-thirds of the world starves while the other one-third over-indulges? What can we do about it? Have you heard of Jubilee 2000? It is an organisation that is campaigning to cancel all Third World debts as a gesture for the millennium. It is based on the biblical idea in Leviticus, Chapter 5, that every fifty years there was a Jubilee year, when all debts were cancelled.

Do you know that for every £1 we give in aid to third world countries we take back £3 in debt repayments?

I hope you signed the Jubilee 2000 petition and got other people to sign it too.

Do you think it is fair that species are dying off at the rate of one every twenty minutes? What can you do about this? We all inhabit this planet and we are all connected to it and to each other so we need to speak up for our fellow travellers. You could hold a 'Council of all Beings' with a group of your friends.

Each of you could go and sit or walk quietly in nature and allow a being to come into your mind. It might be a tree, a plant, an insect, an animal, a forest, etc. Familiarise yourself with your 'being' and begin to see the world from its point of view.

Now come back together for your council meeting and express the views of your being to the meeting. The others will all listen and after each being has spoken, the others say, 'We hear you, snail' (or whatever). You could even make masks and wear the mask of the being who has come to you when you speak. One person could sit in the middle as a human, this position could rotate, but the human does not have a voice on this occasion.

Afterwards you could discuss what it felt like, and decide on a way to make life easier for your particular being.

The following extract is from Chief Seathl's testimony when the American Government wanted to take the land of the Native American Indians. You may be able to find the entire text and read it, it is very beautiful:

> *How can you buy or sell the sky, the warmth of the land? This idea is strange to us.*
> *If we do not own the freshness of the air and the sparkle of the water, how can you buy them?*
> *Every part of this earth is sacred to my people. Every shining pine needle, every sandy shore, every mist in the dark woods, every clearing, and humming insect is holy in the memory and experience of my people. The sap which courses through the trees carries the memories of the red man.*